Rookie
Read-About®
Health

I Have
the Hiccups

by Joanne Mattern

Content Consultant
Catherine A. Dennis, N.P.

Reading Consultant
Jeanne M. Clidas, Ph.D.
Reading Specialist

Children's Press®
An Imprint of Scholastic Inc.

Library of Congress Cataloging-in-Publication Data
Mattern, Joanne, 1963- author.
I have the hiccups/by Joanne Mattern.
    pages cm. — (Rookie read about health)
Summary: "Introduces the reader to hiccups." — Provided by publisher.
Includes index.
ISBN 978-0-531-22706-0 (library binding) — ISBN 978-0-531-22582-0 (pbk.)
    1. Hiccups—Juvenile literature. 2. Reflexes—Juvenile literature. I. Title. II. Series:
Rookie read-about health.
QP372.M38 2016
    612.8'9—dc23   2015021125

Produced by Spooky Cheetah Press
Design by Keith Plechaty

© 2016 by Scholastic Inc.

1 2 3 4 5 6 7 8 9 10 R 25 24 23 22 21 20 19 18 17 16

Photographs ©: cover: Donna Coleman/Thinkstock; 3 top left: BananaStock/
Thinkstock; 3 top right: Fuse/Thinkstock; 3 bottom: bchiku/Thinkstock; 4: 3sbworld/
iStockphoto; 7: Hybrid Images/Media Bakery; 8: Meiko Takechi Arquillos; 11:
gemenacom/iStockphoto; 15: Jon Feingersh Photography_Inc./Media Bakery; 16:
SolStock/iStockphoto; 19: Juanmonino/Thinkstock; 20: Saturated/iStockphoto; 23:
KidStock/Media Bakery; 24: Ariel Skelley/Media Bakery; 27: Laurence Mouton/Media
Bakery; 28: edgardr/iStockphoto; 29: Meiko Takechi Arquillos; 30: Fuse/Thinkstock;
31 center top: Tom Le Goff/Thinkstock; 31 bottom: Saturated/iStockphoto.

Illustrations by Jeffrey Chandler/Art Gecko Studios!

Table of Contents

What Is That Sound?

You feel a funny pain in your throat. *Hic!* You make a weird sound. *Hic!* You have the hiccups!

Hiccups can be a little painful. They might even be embarrassing. But they are nothing to worry about. Everyone gets the hiccups once in a while.

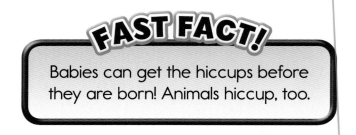

FAST FACT!

Babies can get the hiccups before they are born! Animals hiccup, too.

How Hiccups Happen

Hiccups happen because of a problem with your **diaphragm**. The diaphragm is a big muscle at the bottom of your chest. It helps you to breathe.

This child has his hand on his diaphragm.

When you breathe in, your diaphragm moves down.
That helps pull air into your lungs.
When you breathe out, the diaphragm relaxes and moves up.
Air flows out of your nose and mouth.

Taking a deep breath of fresh air can make you feel great!

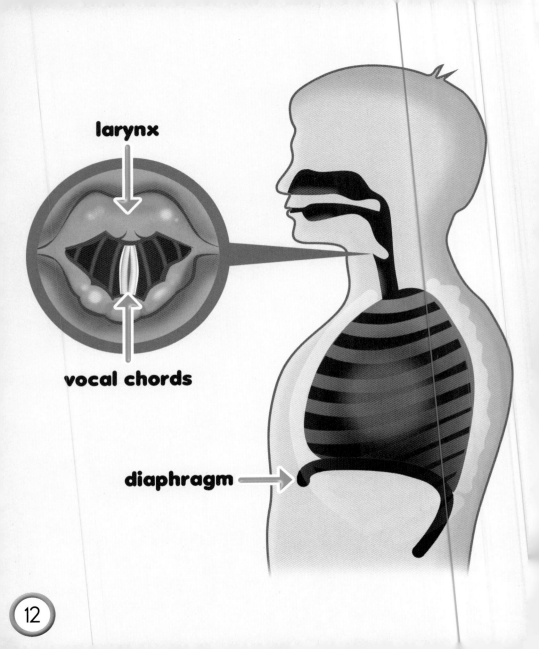

larynx

vocal chords

diaphragm

Sometimes the diaphragm gets **irritated**. When this happens, the diaphragm pulls down quickly. Air rushes into your throat. The air hits your **larynx**.

This illustration shows the parts of your body affected when you hiccup.

When the air hits your larynx, the vocal cords inside snap closed. The vocal cords make a funny sound. That is a hiccup!

Sometimes you get the hiccups if you eat too fast. Sometimes you get them if you try to talk and eat at the same time.

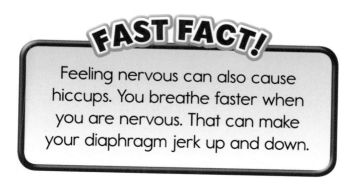

FAST FACT!

Feeling nervous can also cause hiccups. You breathe faster when you are nervous. That can make your diaphragm jerk up and down.

Make It Stop!

Most of the time, hiccups stop in a few minutes. Sometimes they last longer. You can try a few different **remedies** to get rid of hiccups.

Do not be too upset if you get the hiccups. There are things you can do!

Some people think that one way
to stop hiccups is to drink water
out of the wrong side of the glass.
Or put a paper towel over the
glass and drink through it.
Drinking this way takes longer.
It lets your diaphragm calm down.

Some people swallow
a spoonful of sugar
to stop hiccups.

Another way to stop hiccups
is to change your breathing.
You can hold your breath.
Or have someone scare you.
That will make you gasp.

Preventing the Hiccups

Everyone gets the hiccups. But there are ways you can try to avoid them. Remember to eat slowly. Do not try to talk and eat at the same time.

If you feel like you are going to hiccup, take a deep breath. Do not talk or eat. Let your diaphragm calm down and you will feel that funny hiccup go away!

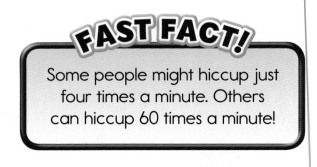

FAST FACT!

Some people might hiccup just four times a minute. Others can hiccup 60 times a minute!

Match each word to its meaning.

1. larynx
2. hiccup
3. diaphragm

a. a muscle that helps you breathe

b. what happens when the diaphragm is irritated

c. a part of your throat

ur your hand at the bottom of your chest, betw
ur ribs. That is your diaphragm. Take a deep
reath in. Now breathe out. Can you feel your
aphragm moving up and down?

Strange but True!

A farmer named Charles Osborne had the longest case of the hiccups. He hiccuped for 68 years!

People have tried all sorts of crazy cures for hiccups. Would you try any of these?

- Drink pickle juice.
- Pull on your tongue.
- Do a handstand.
- Touch your elbows together behind your back.

Just for Fun

Q: What is green and can jump a mile a minute?

A: A frog with the hiccups!

Q: What do you call a mountain with the hiccups?

A: A volcano!

Glossary

diaphragm (DYE-uh-fram): wall of muscle between your chest and your abdomen

irritated (IHR-uh-tay-ted): made sore or sensitive

larynx (LA-ringks): upper part of the windpipe that holds the vocal cords

remedies (REM-uh-deez): things that relieve pain or cure a disease

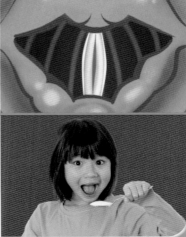

Index

Facts for Now

Visit this Scholastic Web site for more information on hiccups:
www.factsfornow.scholastic.com
Enter the keyword **Hiccups**

About the Author

Joanne Mattern is the author of many nonfiction books for children. She thinks eating a spoonful of sugar is the best way to get rid of hiccups. She lives in New York State with her husband, four children, and numerous pets.